Music CD included with book purchase.

To receive your recording of author Danice Sweet and her group, Revival, singing her songs, which include "He Makes Me Laugh" from this book, fill out the coupon and mail it to the address below. The price of this CD is included in the price of the book.

PLEASE PRINT

Name: _____

Street Address: _____

City, State, Zip Code: _____

MAIL TO:
Pearson Publishing Company
555 S. Shoreline Blvd., Suite 104
Corpus Christi, Texas 78401

He Makes Me Laugh

Words, Music and Drawings
By
Danice E. Sweet

Pearson Publishing Company
Corpus Christi
2010

Copyright © 2010 by Danice E. Sweet

All rights reserved. No part of this book may be reproduced or transmitted in any form or by any means, electronic or mechanical, including photocopy, recording, or any information and storage and retrieval system, without prior written permission from the publisher, except by a reviewer who may quote brief passages in a review.

Library of Congress Control Number: 2010926857

ISBN-13: 978-0-9843326-6-3 paperback

ISBN-13: 978-0-9843326-7-0 e-book

Cover Art: Danice Sweet and Tamara Teas
Cover design: Katherine Pearson Jagoe Massey
Book design: Katherine Pearson Jagoe Massey
Cover production: Tamara Teas, IDS Consulting
Photo on opposite page: Danice Sweet
Photos on pages 59 & 61: Chet Sweet

Published by
Pearson Publishing Company
Corpus Christi, Texas
www.PearsonPub.US

In Loving Memory of
Dr. Gloria Clover, My Mom

Dr. Clover took her second grade classes to the Sedgwick County Zoo every year for over twenty years.

The last time she took her great-grandsons to the zoo (the two boys featured in this book, Gabriel and Noah), a lady walked up to her and said, "Mrs. Clover, you were my second grade teacher, and you brought me here!" Mom was thrilled. She knew she had made a difference in that lady's life.

Danice Sweet

ACKNOWLEDGMENTS

Special thanks to my loving husband, Chet Sweet.
His encouragement and continuous love keep me going.

And also, special thanks to Christine Beaty, my niece, for doing such a great job on our website. Love you, Kiddo!

revivalsinginggroup.com

D. Sweet
2010

Other Books by Danice E. Sweet

Floating Zoo and the Whale Motel

Consider It Joy

I Will Speak Your Name

Published by Pearson Publishing Company, Corpus Christi

He

Makes Me

Laugh

He makes me laugh,

And He makes me sing

My God made everything

He made the monkey and the coconut

He made the palm tree, too

He made the ocean and the octopus

And He made me and you

He makes me laugh

And He makes me sing

He gives me everything I need

He even made the air I breathe

My God made everything

He made the moose

And the mountain goat

He made the rivers, too

He made the forest and the antelope

And He made me and you

He makes me laugh

And He makes me sing

He gives me everything I need

He even made the air I breathe

My God made everything

He made the leopard

He made the elephant

He made the cockatoo

He made the tiger

And orangutan

And He made me and you

The armadillo and the prairie dog

He made the cactus too

The roadrunner and the porcupine

And He made the skunk

too,

peeeeuuuuw!!!!!!

He makes me laugh

And He makes me sing

He gives me everything I need

He even made the air I breathe

My God made everything

What makes *you* smile?

The author's great-nephews: Gabriel (in back) and Noah (in front).

Artist's Workshop

By

Danice E. Sweet

Now it's your turn!
This part of the book is for the artist in each of you.

I always start with a drawing. Usually in pencil. Sometimes while looking at a photograph or even an I-phone picture. Next, I outline the pencil with a thin, black marker.

Then, I decide on what colors I want to use and start painting. Now it's your turn. You can color in the top picture any way you like. What would be in your sky?

Watercolors are put on in layers. I start lightly and then, as I add more layers, the picture gets darker. This painting ended up with seven layers, then I added color and white for the flowers.

I usually start by painting the neutrals: light browns and tan colors.

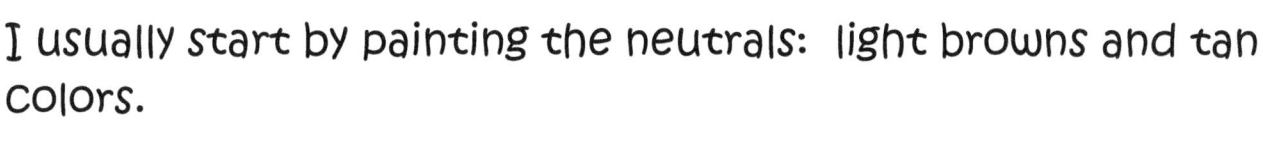

What would you start with first? What colors really jump out at you in the painting on the bottom?

Next, I start adding brighter colors and shading ears and the underside of the trees.

Backgrounds make a difference. I decided to show you what this painting would look like without a background, so I painted it last.

I chose green for the background because I think of tigers in the jungle. I used watercolors and sprinkled on salt, while it was still wet, to help give it a different feeling. What kind of background would you have added?

Draw what makes *you* laugh?

Author and Artist, Danice Sweet, works on a drawing for this book.

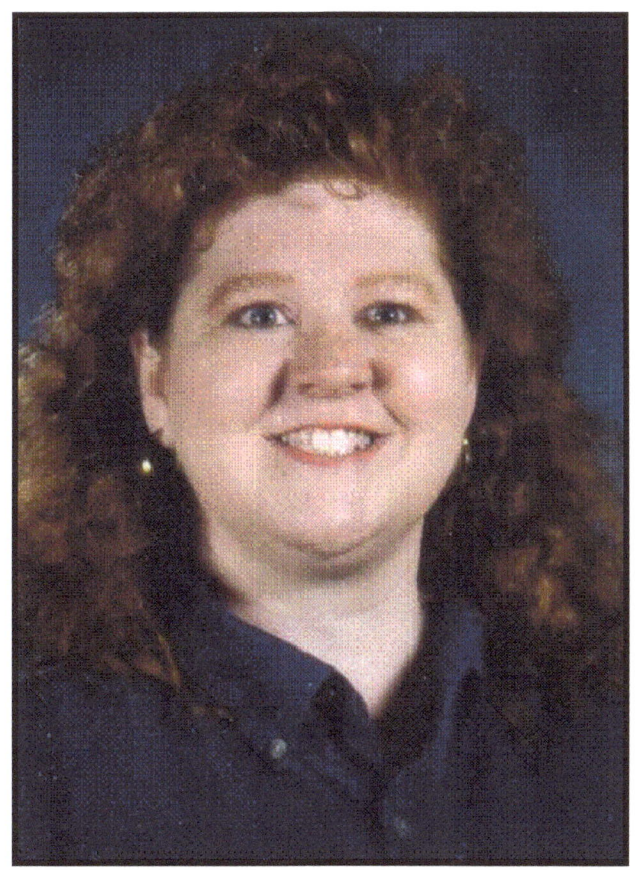

Danice E. Sweet

Mrs. Sweet is not only an illustrator, but also a teacher of art in the public schools, a songwriter, and a singer. She and her singing group "Revival" present concerts around the world. She has been an art teacher for more than twenty years. She has written four books and recorded numerous CD's of her music and that of other composers. For information on her recordings go to her website at revivalsinginggroup.com, and to order her books write to Pearson Publishing Company in Corpus Christi, Texas.

PEARSON PUBLISHING COMPANY
CORPUS CHRISTI, TEXAS

For a complete list and description of our publications and to order books, please go to our website:
www.PearsonPub.US

Saga of a Comanche Warrior
By Max Oliver
Book One: Little Boy $12.95
Book Two: No More $9.95
Book Three: Tomo Pui $9.95
Book Four: Red Nose $9.95
Book Five: Chief Red Nose $10.95

Slumbertime: A Parent's Guide for Children's Sleep and Sleep Problems
By Janet S. Gould $29.95

Catching the Dream: A Parent's Guide for Children's Dreams
By Janet S. Gould $26.95

Deal Me In
By Alyce Guynn with illustrations by Jesse Taylor $23.95

His Angels Are In Charge
By Frances Cotten Woodard $24.95

Floating Zoo and the Whale Motel
Written and illustrated by Danice Sweet $26.95

Consider It Joy
Written and illustrated by Danice Sweet $16.95

I Will Speak Your Name
Written and Illustrated by Danice Sweet $16.95

To mail in orders, send (1) a list of titles with number of copies of each title, (2) check or money order for total retail price of all books, plus (3) $5.00 shipping and handling for each book and (4) your name and mailing address, printed clearly, to:

Pearson Publishing Company
555 S. Shoreline Blvd., Suite 104
Corpus Christi, Texas 78401

Use these pages for your drawings.

www.ingramcontent.com/pod-product-compliance
Lightning Source LLC
Chambersburg PA
CBHW040054160426
43192CB00002B/67